A BOOK OF BIRDS,
DREAMS,
AND OTHER THINGS

By Walter Bauer

ISBN-13: 978-0615770109
ISBN-10: 061577010x

For Barrett, Tanner,
And Dashiell

WATCHING

Turn your gaze up to the sky
In the awakening light
A bird does fly

Flapping, rising, turning, gliding
Swooping, soaring, on clear wind riding

You can look with your eyes
For visions enlightening
You can watch with your heart
Where dreams are hiding

A PLACE TO SHARE

We all live in different places
With different weather
Seeing all kinds of faces

Parents go to work almost every day
While children go to school or play

We need a place to have a meal
To lay down and rest
To share with family and friends
The place called home is the best

WINDOWS

Windows are for looking out
To see what the day is all about

When the sun is bright and the birds are singing
We want to be out in the light
Moving and playing

When the rain does fall and the wind does howl
We want to be warm and safe from it all

CLOCKS

Clocks tell time, and the time does fly
We hope to grow big and strong
And learn the reasons why

With the sun on our shoulders we are happy
And then
The darkness comes, and the moon is our friend

The days go around; we may grow a little wise
The clock says, "It's soon…"
But time always flies

THE ROBIN

The robin is a familiar friend
In the morning you just might see him again

With his reddish breast and his coat of brown
You often find him hopping around

On your lawn when the grass is wet with dew
Looking for breakfast, maybe a worm or two

RUNNING

When you are running hard and fast
You see things in a blur, rushing past

Some are so fast, they almost can't be caught
But one thing you may have already been taught

Is that you can go far if you slow down a bit
And breathe a little easier, but never quit

SPIDER WEB

The spider like a magician spins
A web to catch his dinner in

The fly is doomed when it gets stuck here
The spider will wrap it up
And make it disappear

But the web is also a thing of beauty
Catching the light
Strung with diamonds of dew
In the morning bright

WINTER

Winter's a time when the air is most often cold
Leaves have fallen
And the wind is bold

The sky is grey
Filled with snow or rain
You might wonder when it will be warm out again

Bundled up in your coat you might go
For a stroll in the cold air
To find a piece of blue sky
Fallen in a puddle somewhere

CATS AND DOGS

When a dog and a cat meet
Sometimes this is what you'll see
The dog will run and bark
And the cat will flee

As fast as it can
Perhaps right up a tree
Leaving the dog to sit there
Barking unhappily

Does the dog want to eat the cat?
Does it want to play?
The cat doesn't want to find out
In its tree it will stay

DREAMS IN DAY AND NIGHT

Sometimes you dream in the day
Even with your eyes open
You think of things to wish for
Picture what you hope will happen

Sometimes when you dream at night
You think of other things
Those that are strange, or even frightening

But darkness will sink, and the sun will rise
Your heart will feel light
When you open your eyes

THE JAY

The jay, with his coat of blue and his crest
Always acts like he knows exactly what's best

Loud and shrill are what his squawk is
Some people think he's pesky and obnoxious

Is he bragging? complaining? putting on a show?
"I'm as fresh as the air," he's letting you know

BALLS

Most balls you can describe
By saying they are round
Though in sizes and colors they do abound

When one fits in your hand just exactly right
You can throw it as far as you can
With all of your might

But one of the nicest things
That with a ball you can do
Is to play catch with someone
And have them throw it back to you

CHAIRS

Chairs are for sitting on
Have no doubt
They're not for standing or jumping on
Or fooling about

If you lean too far back
When you're in your chair
You'll find yourself with your feet
Pointing up into the air

You'll land on the floor
With quite a smack
And maybe even hurt your back

GARDEN

A garden is a place for things to grow
That you have planted and tended
And come to know

There is a bush, here is a tree
That will bear some fruit in the spring, you see

And with some rain showers
And of course the sunshine
The fresh beauty of flowers
Will be yours and mine

YOUR FACE

Below your hair and above your nose
Your eyes to the world you do expose

Below your nose and above your chin
A mouth for talking, and putting food in

On each side is an ear – you can listen if you try
To the song of the birds, to the wind in the sky

YOUR FACE (#2)

In the mirror you see
A familiar face
With moods and expressions
That travel all over the place

Do you like what you see?
I hope that you do
Be kind to others
But be kind to yourself, too

And as you travel the world
Mile after mile
People will always be glad
To see you smile

DRAGONFLIES

Dragonflies go whirring through the air
So big and quick
They might give you a scare

But if you see one land
With its shimmering wings
And big eyes and long body
What a wondrous thing!

They won't bite or sting you
So let them be
To hover and dart
And dance for you and me

BEDTIME

At night when the sky is black and clear
The moon and his friends the stars appear

The moon in all his quiet phases
And the stars with all their twinkling gazes

Will watch over you and make it all right
Until the hills are touched with morning light

BEDTIME (#2)

Sometimes at day's end
When it's time for bed
You don't want to go
So you have to be led

By your Mom or your Dad
And they'll tell you a story
Or sing you a song
To make the night less scary

And though the day was fun
Now you must rest
In the quiet of night
By a dream you'll be blessed

THE MOURNING DOVE

The mourning dove, on whispering wings
Flies through the twilight
Then she lands and she sings

With voice and heart that are tender and true
She calls out with longing
"Coo-ah, coo, coo, coo"

She's not asking a question of me or of you
But singing for the night
So lonely and blue

THE CROW

One of nature's comedians, as you might know
Is the clever, loud-voiced bird known as the crow

From up on a wire or up in a tree
He calls, jeering and joking about you and me

And about all of us humans in a world oft absurd
He cries, "I'm so lucky and glad just to be a bird!"

MOUNTAINS AND RIVERS

The mountains whose great and rocky
Shoulders rub the sky
Catch the rain and snow from clouds
As they go passing by

In the trickling of rain
And silent melting of snow
Are the beginnings of a river
And the river will grow

Pouring through valleys and fields
Past houses and trees
Water rushing and rolling
Back to the sea

THE OCEAN

You might go to the beach
On a nice sunny day
To play in the sand
To wade in the waves

Across blue-green water
You just might spy
Some boats or an ocean liner
Sailing by

And if you take home a sea shell
Hold it up to your ear
A whispering echo of the waves
You might be able to hear

POTS AND PANS AND DISHES

All these things in the kitchen
For cooking and serving
A meal of which you are most deserving

For on a day filled with hard work
And good honest play
You need something to keep you strong
And well on the way

But before you dig into
Your bowl or your plate-full
Take a moment to show
That you are truly grateful

TELEVISION

Television's a box that makes pictures and noise
It might seem to be a most magical toy

It shows things that are real
And things make believe
Stories that might teach you
Or that just might deceive

If you observe people watching TV
It might seem
That they are hypnotized
Or living in a dream

THE EAGLE

The eagle of grand and lofty flight
Has sharp beak and talons, and keen eyesight

Sometimes a hunter of small animals and birds
Sometimes he flies just to be lord of his world

Swaying and soaring on currents of air
From high in the blue he can see everywhere

CLOUDS

High overhead, floating effortlessly
Are the shifting, changing clouds
Mysterious and free

If you pick out a cloud
And watch it drift through the sky
It will remind you of things
Changing shape all the while

Clouds like cotton, like feathers
Clouds fast and clouds slow
Clouds white, grey, and pink
Strange creatures on the go

SHOES

Shoes are funny and useful things
When they are new they seem to have wings

Day after day
Over dirt, grass, and street
They grow dusty and worn
Protecting your feet

At night, with aching soles
And their tongues hanging out
They dream of tomorrow
And running and leaping about

HANDS

Among all the animals it's easy to see
That humans can use their hands most cleverly

With fingers nimble and quick
And a touch that's precise
They play and do tricks
And work that's ever so nice

When someone's sad or in need
Or maybe just a good friend
Sometimes you want to hold their hand

TEDDY AND FRIENDS

We all have friends who are not human at all
Perhaps a stuffed teddy bear or maybe a doll

They've seen all of our moods
And watched as we grow
Watched us dreaming at night
In the moon's tender glow

And sometimes when it seems
That something's missing
You can tell them a story
And they'll always listen

SUMMER – SPRINKLERS

In summer the sun's hot and lazy
Drifting slowly over earth
You might sit under a tree
Enjoying shade for all it's worth

Or, if your parents say it's all right
You might turn on a sprinkler
And play in the light

Light sparkling off water so cool wet and fine
You leap and dance on the grass
And have a wonderful time

CARS

When riding in a car
You can see the world passing by
Sometimes it seems so far to go
You have to let out a sigh

You wish you were there already
But of course you must know
That Mom or Dad will get you
Where you have to go

So you might hum a tune
Through sun, rain, or snow
The world passes by
Sometimes fast, sometimes slow

BRIDGES AND TUNNELS

Bridges are built for going over
A bay, a canyon, a river
You'll find yourself up in the air
Sometimes so high you shiver

Tunnels are built for going through
In a car or train you might ride
Into darkness, going underground
Or through a mountainside

Birds have this advantage
Being commanders of the air:
They don't have to build a thing
Wherever they want, they just fly there

WIND

Seldom warm, often cold
He races through the leaves
And ripples the water, shakes at the eaves

Sometimes silently breezing
Sometimes howling out loud
Swirling sand and dust, and hurrying the clouds

An invisible traveler of spaces and lands
He touches our faces
And slips through our hands

GREAT BLUE HERON

With long thin legs
The blue heron can be seen wading
In the shallow water
Of lakes and tidelands, feeding

On water-creatures he catches
With a swift jab of his bill
And if you watch for a while
You will have the thrill

Of seeing him rise to the air
Great wings beating slow
And take off over the water
Flying graceful and low

FALLING LEAVES

In autumn the days get shorter
The sun seems pale and cool
The children who are old enough
Are busy back at school

The air is crisp and fresh
And when the wind moves through the trees
It brings to life fiery colors
Of the changing leaves

Orange, yellow, red:
The hues of sunset do abound
Then the leaves come loose
Swirl and flutter to the ground

HALLOWEEN

At a certain time of year
Many monsters roam the night
Vampires, ghosts, and Frankensteins
Enough to give someone a fright

Witches, devils, and pirates
And very hungry too
Perhaps a Cinderella
Or the lucky prince who found her shoe

In the light of Jack-o-lanterns
A'trick-or-treating they will go
Who are these little monsters?
It's a secret we all know

OWL

They say the owl is very wise
And knows just what to do
In darkness he can see quite well
And his hearing is sharp, too

A hunter and a watcher
He waits patiently in his tree
With big round eyes he finds his prey
Then swoops down so quietly

As the moon climbs high, and the forest darkens
He will give you a clue:
When spirits of the night go passing by
He calls out, "WHO goes there, WHO?"

BIRTHDAY

Once a year and only once
Comes this day especially for you
When people will sing out your name
And give you presents, too

Though you can't remember your own birth
Your parents certainly do
And in their hearts they celebrate
The wonder that is you

Maybe you'll get a special meal
And cake with candles, too
Think of happiness for those you love
And hope the wish comes true

GAMES

Some games you play to win or lose
Some games are like a test
But most are just to pass the time
Having fun is what is best

Some games you play with many people
In the lively sun and air
Some games you play with one good friend
Someone you're glad is there

Some games you play just by yourself
Sometimes you are alone
Then you can use your imagination
The rules are all your own

TREES

The branches of a tree reach up and out
And from them grow the leaves
That catch the wind and sun
In green and changing ease

Trees are home to birds and squirrels
And other animals in the wild
Sometimes a tree is a place to climb
For a cat, or a careful child

Up in a tree the sky shines through
In little blue moving pieces
The world below is far away
You're riding on the breezes

BATH TIME

When you're done with being outside
At the end of another busy day
It's time to get all nice and clean
Taking a bath is a good way

In the water, with some soap you scrub
Off the dirt and grime
And if you have toys to play with
You have a good way to pass the time

Maybe a boat, a duck, a whale
Some characters from TV
You can play a game, splash and sing
And get real clean quite happily

END OF THE YEAR

On a chilly December eve
The wind scurries down the street
But the kitchen's cozy and fine
With the smell of something good to eat

All bundled up you might go
With your parents for a stroll or a ride
Houses decorated with colored lights
Windows looking warm inside

And visit a neighbor or a friend
To share in some talk and good cheer
Be thankful for having people to love
And hope for a happy new year

YOUNG DOGS RUNNING

On a hill or a field
Where you can let your dogs run free
They go racing and bounding so happily

Like clouds need the wind, like birds need the air
Young dogs need time to run and play
With hardly any care

And their spirits will be free
Their spirits will roam
But soon you'll have to call them
Because it will be time to go home

AIRPLANE

Perhaps you have already
Perhaps one day you will
Take a ride in an airplane
It's really quite a thrill

To fly in such a big metal bird
High above the earth
And if you can sit by a window
Watch for all you're worth:

Patterns of water and land, far below
Like a huge and colorful map
Or maybe just a sea of clouds
Above the clouds is where you're at

STORMY NIGHT

The rain on the roof, on a stormy night
Makes us feel so small
We float on rivers of dreams, lost it seems
And the wind through the trees does howl

In the morning when we awaken
We find that our world is still here
But the leaves are shiny, the earth is wet
And rich new smells are in the air

And when the sun finally emerges
From behind its clouds of grey
The hills are green, the birds singing:
For this we thank the rain

THE WAYS OF DREAMS

Some dreams stay in memory
More often they just flee
Back into the night from where they came
Leaving you with mystery

Some dreams are a lot like real life
Most are rather strange
Some dreams give you good advice
How your life you might rearrange

A dream can take you on a journey
To a place you've never been
You might come to a door that was locked before
And hear a voice say, "Come right on in"

GROWING UP

Trees grow up into the world
Through seasons of the year
In golden fall, in spring so bold
Under summer skies deep blue and clear

Boys and girls grow in a whirl
Of things to do and learn
Crawling, walking, running, jumping
With energy to burn

Children: listen to the trees
See the world in all its turning
You need a heart that's firmly rooted
Skies of hope and yearning

WHEN YOU ARE SAD

You don't always get to choose
Things don't always go your way
The game might end too early
Maybe there's no one to play with today

Maybe somebody hurt your feelings
Accidentally or on purpose
Maybe your heart's in disrepair
In need of special service

Maybe you need some quiet time
A good night's sleep and new awakening
Maybe you need someone to talk to
Someone who loves you is ready and waiting

HUMMINGBIRD

The little hummingbird
Does things no other bird can do
He hovers in one place
And flies straight up and backwards, too

As he maneuvers like a helicopter
You hear him hum and whir
Tiny wings moving so fast
They seem just like a blur

His specialty is to hang in the air
By a flower so delicately
And reach in with his slender bill
To drink the nectar, oh so tasty

GROWING UP (#2)

Sometimes you must push hard forward
Sometimes wait your turn
Sometimes you must ask a question
Sometimes listen and learn

Make the world a little better
Don't be afraid to try
Imagine there are answers
Let your dreams roam far and wide

Appreciate those who care for you
Show them that you do
Let love be the well you draw from
To your love be true

www.ingramcontent.com/pod-product-compliance
Lightning Source LLC
Chambersburg PA
CBHW042008150426
43195CB00002B/58